"Sound the shofar for our freedom."[1c]
— when was the last biblical Jubilee year? (You may need to look up online...... :))

Mysteries
of Mary

THE
FULLNESS OF
DISCIPLESHIP

Be[...]

LIG[...]

||||||||||||||||||||||||||
D1002669

Email me anytime!

aromand4@
    tcnj.edu

or call/text (of course!)

Liguori
ONE LIGUORI DRIVE
LIGUORI MO 63057-9999
314.464.2500

(609)
556-
0964.

Imprimi Potest:
Richard Thibodeau, C.SS.R.
Provincial, Denver Province
The Redemptorists

Imprimatur:
Most Reverend Michael J. Sheridan
Auxiliary Bishop, Archdiocese of St. Louis

ISBN 0-7648-0356-5
Library of Congress Catalog Card Number: 98-67383

Scripture quotations from the *New Revised Standard Ver-
sion of the Bible*, © 1989 by the Division of Christian Educa-
tion of the National Council of the Churches of Christ in the
USA. Used with permission. All rights reserved.

This is a revised edition of a book originally titled *Mary and
Your Everyday Life: A Book of Meditations*, © 1977, Liguori
Publications.

Cover design by Wendy Barnes

Table *of* Contents

The Annunciation

IN THE SIXTH MONTH
the angel Gabriel was sent by God to a town in Galilee called Nazareth, to a virgin engaged to a man whose name was Joseph, of the house of David. The virgin's name was Mary. And he came to her and said, "Greetings, favored one! The Lord is with you."

But she was much perplexed by his words and pondered what sort of greeting this might be.

The angel said to her, "Do not be afraid, Mary, for you have found favor with God. And now, you will conceive in your womb and bear a son, and you will name him Jesus. He will be great, and will be called the Son of the Most High, and the Lord God will give to him the throne of his ancestor David. He will reign over the house of Jacob forever, and of his kingdom there will be no end."

Mary said to the angel, "How can this be, since I am a virgin?"

The angel said to her, "The Holy Spirit will come upon you, and the power of the Most High will overshadow you; therefore the child to be born will be holy; he will be called Son of God. And now, your relative Elizabeth in her old age has also conceived a son; and this is the sixth month for her who was said to be barren. For nothing will be impossible with God."

Then Mary said, "Here am I, the servant of the Lord; let it be with me according to your word."

Then the angel departed from her.

Luke 1:26-38

1. Mary: Sign of Hope

"THE LORD IS WITH YOU."

"Therefore the Lord himself will give you a sign. Look, the young woman is with child and shall bear a son, and shall name him Immanuel" (ISAIAH 7:14).

The first pages of Holy Scripture underline the equal dignity of woman and man: *Then God said, "Let us make humankind in our image, according to our likeness."…So God created humankind in his image, in the image of God he created them; male and female he created them* (GENESIS 1:26A, 27).

As men and women complement each other, mutually making up what is lacking in each, we follow the new Adam and the new Eve, trying to become ever more fully an image and likeness of God, making visible for each other the presence of "God-with-us."

We share in this great mission to be an image of God for each other: an image of God's fidelity, goodness, and tender love. We must cry out in pain, seeing how we betray our dignity instead of receiving each other as God's gift and praising God in concert. We are self-centered, concealing more often than revealing God.

But God's promise is with us from the very beginning. There will come a new Adam and a new Eve. The woman is a sign of hope: *The LORD God said to the serpent…. "I will put enmity between you and the woman, and between your offspring and hers; he will strike your head, and you will strike his heel"* (GENESIS 3:14A, 15).

The victor over arrogant and evil spirits is Jesus Christ, the new Adam; but the promise of the Savior is introduced by the image of the humble and courageous woman who is set as a sign against the evil one, against all those who in their arrogance and pride refuse to adore God and will not love their neighbors. This child is the visible image of the invisible God: *For a child has been born for us, a son given to us; authority rests upon his shoulders; and he is named Wonderful Counselor, Mighty God, Everlasting Father, Prince of Peace* (Isaiah 9:6).

Mary, the new Eve, is companion to Jesus in her humility and purity. Mary surely lives most intensely the charism of the virgin who lives fully in vigilant waiting for the coming of the Lord. The oil in her lamp is burning; all her being longs for the Lord in readiness to greet him when he comes.

If we want to truly venerate Mary, we need to appreciate the charism of vigilance and readiness.

Blessed are we if we follow Mary in her vigilance and readiness.

O Mary,
whenever we remember you and call upon your name,
we feel hope in us and long to know with you
     the Immanuel—
the experience of God's nearness.
We thank you for your fervent prayer,
for your longing that was fulfilled in the coming
     of our Savior.
Pray for us,
that our lives may be a constant thanksgiving
     for his coming
and become for many a sign of hope and of trust,
and an invitation to seek the Lord.

2. Mary: Full of Grace

"GREETINGS, FAVORED ONE!"

The fullness of time has come. The sign of the promise, the virgin, is now manifest to us. Her name is Mary. Hers is the privileged name of God's design, a name that fills our heart with trust and joy.

With God's angel, we say, "Greetings." This is the way we speak to her in our Hail Mary; we might also translate the word as "Rejoice." It is God who invites Mary to rejoice for the coming of the Messianic era. How could she not rejoice, knowing that she is the promised sign that announces the coming of the Prince of Peace? Each time we greet her with the Hail Mary, we join in her joy and gratitude.

She is "favored"; God has graced her. She belongs totally to the Servant of Yahweh of whom the Lord spoke, through the prophet: *Here is my servant, whom I uphold, my chosen, in whom my soul delights* (ISAIAH 42:1A).

The greeting that comes from God is a mighty word. We may say it is an effective sacramental sign. Through a special revelation, Mary comes to know that she is a sign that God fulfills his promises to Israel, as she tells us: *"…according to the promise he made to our ancestors, to Abraham and to his descendants forever"* (LUKE 1:55).

From beginning to end, the life of Mary is graced; for she renders thanks always and everywhere, and thus she is open to experience the Lord's graciousness and to respond with generosity and ever greater gratitude. Grace *(charis)* is not a thing. It is God's attractive love, manifested to Mary and to all of us, in order to draw us to the very heart of God.

"The Lord is with you." Now the great moment of history has come when the virgin will uniquely learn and understand the name, *Immanuel.* Surprised by the newness of the revelation, Mary needs help to overcome all fear and entrust herself totally to God, to touch the grace she is gifted with. She remains in the Lord's grace because she is forever humble, grateful, and faithful.

"Do not be afraid, Mary." God's presence, and the revelation that the moment of fulfillment of the ancient promises has come, shakes Mary's whole being. The angel calls him God with *us,* in view of *all* of us. Her heart overflows with joy, and yet she is shaken by her holy fear of God. Mary rejoices in the Lord's nearness, and praises the holy Name of God. And she—the daughter of Israel—does not think only about herself. Her joy in the presence of the Savior is our joy, and we join her in her praise and thanksgiving.

Blessed are we if we follow Mary's example of humility, gratefulness, and faithfulness.

O Mary,
what a joy it is that we can greet you with the words,
    "full of grace"!
The favor you have found is for all of us;
the Lord, who is with you, comes to be with all of us.
We shall experience that if, like you, we are faithful
    and grateful.
Pray for us
that we may always be able to rejoice in the Lord's
    presence.

3. Mary: Virgin and Mother

"AND NOW, YOU WILL CONCEIVE IN YOUR WOMB AND BEAR A SON, AND YOU WILL NAME HIM JESUS."..."HOW CAN THIS BE, SINCE I AM A VIRGIN?"

Mary, the most humble among the humble, the holiest among all the saints, believes that the promised Messiah will be the "Servant of God." Now, she comes to know the great mystery: the One whom she will call Jesus ("God our Savior") is the Son of the Most High and his reign will have no end. She is the mother privileged to give him the name, a name which she experiences within her being. As mother, she will sing the praise of the Servant of God. As mother, she will give him loving care, and as believer, she will adore him.

Mary shares with her people a memory filled with gratitude for the wonderful things God has done throughout the centuries. The memory now becomes a total celebration of gratitude for the promise brought to fulfillment in her son, destined to be Savior and Lord of all the world. Through the special grace of the Holy Spirit, all that has transpired reaches its summit. What has happened becomes, for her and through her, God's self-bestowal on humanity. She gives herself totally to the One who is so gracious.

Mary is immaculate. Her life, marked by the law of growth, is more than that of others. Her faith becomes an ever more glorious light. In her openness to the divine message and the gift of herself, she becomes ever more intensely grateful and joyous. God has guided her, step by step, to the moment in which she conceives the Son of the Most High. God's grace has prepared her heart, soul, body, will, and emotional response.

Mary has no doubts that the revelation will be fulfilled. Yet, she humbly asks what her cooperation in this wonderful event will be: *"How can this be, since I am a virgin?"* (LUKE 1:34). It is the prayer of one who lives in faith, but with a fullness and sincerity that makes her the model of the Church. She teaches us how to search for nothing other than to know and to do the will of God. Mary is total openness to the will of God. In that total gift of self, it becomes clear to her that she is the virgin who will call her son Jesus, God-with-us.

Blessed are we if we follow Mary's example of total openness to the will of God.

O Mary,
virgin and mother,
Mother of the Son of God made human in you, and
*   our mother also,*
pray for us
that, like you, we might seek only one thing:
the will of God.
And that we might seek it with that humility and
*   purity of heart*
that distinguishes your faith.

4. Mary's "Yes"

"HERE AM I, THE SERVANT OF THE LORD; LET IT BE WITH ME ACCORDING TO YOUR WORD."

The prophecies that are now to be fulfilled echo in the heart of Mary. *Comfort, O comfort my people, says your God. Speak tenderly to Jerusalem, and cry to her that she has served her term, that her penalty is paid, that she has received from the Lord's hand double for all her sins. A voice cries out: "In the wilderness prepare the way of the LORD, make straight in the desert a highway for our God. Every valley shall be lifted up, and every mountain and hill be made low; the uneven ground shall become level, and the rough places a plain. Then the glory of the LORD shall be revealed, and all people shall see it together, for the mouth of the LORD has spoken"* (ISAIAH 40:1-5).

Now the hour has come, and the fulfillment is greater than anyone could have imagined. *"The Holy Spirit will come upon you, and the power of the Most High will overshadow you; therefore the child to be born will be holy; he will be called Son of God"* (LUKE 1:35). This is the moment of a new creation, a manifestation greater than the creation of the universe from nothingness. This is the moment to which the earth can respond only with silence, adoration, and everlasting thanksgiving.

To confirm the message for Mary, whose faith is already pure and strong, and to enhance our own faith, the angel adds: *"And now, your relative Elizabeth in her old age has also conceived a son; and this is the sixth month for her who was said to be barren. For nothing will be impossible with God"* (LUKE 1:36-37).

Mary responds: *"Here am I, the servant of the Lord;*

let it be with me according to your word" (LUKE 1:38). It is clear to the faith of Mary that she is the companion of Christ, the Servant of God. As the new Eve, she gives her free and grateful assent, thus fulfilling the life and the prayer of all the prophets: "Here I am, Lord, call me; here I am, send me."

Mary's faith and fidelity are accompanied by the revelation of God's power. *And the Word became flesh and lived among us, and we have seen his glory, the glory as of a father's only son, full of grace and truth* (JOHN 1:14).

Blessed are we if we follow Mary's example of free and grateful assent.

O Mary,
Mother of our Lord Jesus Christ,
we thank you for your humble "yes."
You did not want to be anything other than a
*   servant of God,*
following him who is the Servant of God and of all
*   people.*
We rejoice with you,
for the Most High has given you the honor and the
*   joy to be the mother of the Son of God*
who has taken flesh in you.
In our name, too,
you have given the response of faith.
Pray that we may respond, as you,
with all our heart and all our being.

The Visitation

IN THOSE DAYS

Mary set out and went with haste to a Judean town in the hill country, where she entered the house of Zechariah and greeted Elizabeth.

When Elizabeth heard Mary's greeting, the child leaped in her womb.

And Elizabeth was filled with the Holy Spirit and exclaimed with a loud cry, "Blessed are you among women, and blessed is the fruit of your womb. And why has this happened to me, that the mother of my Lord comes to me? For as soon as I heard the sound of your greeting, the child in my womb leaped for joy.

"And blessed is she who believed that there would be a fulfillment of what was spoken to her by the Lord."

Luke 1:39-45

5. Mary Visits Elizabeth

"HERE AM I, THE SERVANT OF THE LORD."

Mary meets Elizabeth and Zechariah. Her greeting is more than a courtesy, or mere joy in the meeting of old friends. She, as the daughter of Zion, extends greetings with the age-old blessing and sign of hope: *shalom*— peace. At this moment, it is the fulfillment of the hope of Israel. Mary bears in her womb the Prince of Peace, who has taken on our human condition to radiate joy and peace in the hearts of all people. Mary's visit and greeting are signs of the coming and blessing of the Lord.

The biblical text makes us consciously aware that Mary's greeting was a powerful prayer and blessing: *When Elizabeth heard Mary's greeting, the child leaped in her womb.* Through Mary, the one chosen to "prepare the way of the Lord" comes in contact with Jesus. His response is exultation, the sign of the peace and joy of the Messianic age.

And Elizabeth was filled with the Holy Spirit and exclaimed with a loud cry, "Blessed are you among women, and blessed is the fruit of your womb." In that favored moment, Elizabeth received the Holy Spirit, inspiration to prophets, who led her to discover the profound meaning of the visit of Mary. Her response is a blessing and a grateful affirmation of what God has done in Mary. Each time we say the Hail Mary, we join in praise for all that God has done in Mary.

Later, John the Baptist will exclaim with astonishment: *"I need to be baptized by you, and do you come to me?"* (MATTHEW 3:14). With that same incredulous humility, Elizabeth now questions: *"And why has this happened to me, that the mother of my Lord comes to me?"* The coming of the servant of the Lord can be welcomed only with deep humility. The coming of Mary inspires veneration and awe, for blessed is the one who comes in the name of the Lord.

In the house of visitation, we see a wonderful dialogue of faith, a shared prayer. There are five persons present: the eternal Word, made human in the womb of the virgin; his mother, who brings the source of all blessing and peace; Elizabeth, filled with the Holy Spirit; the greatest among all the prophets, who prepares the coming of Christ, John the Baptist; and Zechariah, a man of deep silence but with open eyes and heart. His silence is a true participation: listening and presence. The song he sings is "Praise to the God of Israel." Every Christian family/community is called to be a house of prayer, a source of joy for many.

Blessed are we if we follow Mary's example of sharing faith and praising God.

O Mary,
we thank you
with all the people to whose houses you have brought
the blessing and peace of Christ.
Bless us with your greeting,
shalom,
and pray for us
that we may be attentive to the many signs
of the coming of Christ into our life.

6. Mary: Model of Faith

"BLESSED IS SHE WHO BELIEVED THAT THERE WOULD BE A FULFILLMENT OF WHAT WAS SPOKEN TO HER BY THE LORD."

Now faith is the assurance of things hoped for, the conviction of things not seen. Indeed, by faith our ancestors received approval. By faith we understand that the worlds were prepared by the word of God, so that what is seen was made from things that are not visible (HEBREWS 11:1-3).

All the wonderful things of which the Letter to the Hebrews speaks become an even greater song of joy when we think of the faith of Mary: In fullness of faith, Mary perceives the wondrous new creation that happens in the Incarnation of the eternal Word. It is the creation of the new earth and the new heaven, a creation more wonderful than that of the visible universe.

Without faith it is impossible to please God (HEBREWS 11:6). Mary pleases God more than any other creature. She excels by her faith and trust in God. Through faith, Mary becomes the ark of salvation through which the Savior of the world comes to us. She is the model and the promise for the Church (see HEBREWS 11:7).

Mary's faith far surpasses the faith of Abraham and all the patriarchs as well (see HEBREWS 11:8). She is ready to leave all of life's usual patterns behind, setting out into a totally new and unknown land, and accepting the mission to be the mother and deaconess, the servant of the Savior of the world. In faith-like obedience, she accepts the greatest exodus: beyond Egypt and the desert, to the exodus of the cross.

God frees Abraham and his offspring from the pattern of their culture, in which firstborn sons were frequently sacrificed. God does not will the sacrifice of Jesus, God's own son, but only that Jesus make manifest his total readiness to give himself for the salvation of humankind. He does, and he is totally followed by his mother. Mary joins the sacrifice of Christ on the cross of salvation.

Mary exceeds the faith of all people because her total being turns to Jesus. She knows him as the Savior of all and she gives herself totally to him who is the Servant. It is in this way that Mary teaches all of us. In all that she does and says, she reminds us there is no salvation in any other name save in that of Jesus.

And what of us? *Therefore, since we are surrounded by so great a cloud of witnesses, let us also lay aside every weight and the sin that clings so closely, and let us run with perseverance the race that is set before us* (HEBREWS 12:1).

Blessed are we if we follow Mary's example of total and uncompromising faith in Jesus.

O Mary,
each time we pray, "blessed are you among women,"
we praise you on behalf of your faith.
Pray for us
that our faith may always be strong and radiant,
filled with hope
and readiness to become,
with you,
a living gospel,
bringing the Messianic peace to all people.

The
Magnificat

AND MARY SAID,

"My soul magnifies the Lord, and my spirit rejoices in God my Savior, for he has looked with favor on the lowliness of his servant. Surely, from now on all generations will call me blessed; for the Mighty One has done great things for me, and holy is his name. His mercy is for those who fear him from generation to generation. He has shown strength with his arm; he has scattered the proud in the thoughts of their hearts. He has brought down the powerful from their thrones, and lifted up the lowly; he has filled the hungry with good things, and sent the rich away empty. He has helped his servant Israel, in remembrance of his mercy, according to the promise he made to our ancestors, to Abraham and to his descendants forever."

Luke 1:46-55

7. Mary's Song of Praise

**"MY SOUL MAGNIFIES THE LORD, AND MY SPIRIT RE-
JOICES IN GOD MY SAVIOR."**

Mary is truly Israel, the servant, the humble handmaid
who can sing the song of faith and joy, the Song of the
Servant that will be fulfilled in Jesus, her son. If we
meditate on the Songs of the Servant in Second Isaiah
(42:1-4; 49:1-7; 50:4-11; 52:13—53:12), and then upon
the Magnificat, we see the spiritual unity. Thus, Scripture tells us that Mary is the new Eve—Israel in its best—
and she is truly on the side of the hoped-for Messiah,
the Servant of God.

Surely, Mary lives the Song of the Servant and shares
it with Elizabeth and Zechariah. But it is not merely a
song in one great peak experience; it is the word and
prayer displayed so lavishly by the totality of her life,
thoughts, desires, and actions. In the hours of joy and in
the moments of suffering—even under the cross—
Mary's life sings the Song of the Servant. Mary *is* the
Magnificat. The apostolic community finds in this great
song of praise a perfect blend of the life and the role of
Mary in the Church.

The Magnificat expresses more than just the personal
faith of Mary and her most intimate union with God. It
is the life-song of the one whom we honor as our model.
Mary's life manifests what is meant to be the role of the
Church throughout salvation history, enabling the
Church to proclaim that God is on the side of the little
ones. It is God who humbles the arrogant and exalts his
Servant, Jesus Christ, and all those who follow him, after the example of Mary.

Mary is totally consecrated to the adoration and

praise of God who is manifested in the fullness of her being. Her life is thanksgiving. She is, with Jesus and in view of Jesus, the perfect eucharistic person. As adorer of the Father "in spirit and in truth," part of her thankful adoration is her sensitivity to the needs of others and her desire to bring the Good News of salvation to all people, thus honoring and praising God.

"My spirit rejoices in God my Savior" could also be translated: "My spirit rejoices in Jesus," for the name Jesus, "Joshua" in Hebrew, means literally "God my Savior." The spirit of Mary is touched and moved by the Holy Spirit. In her life is fulfilled the prophecy of Ezekiel: *"I will put my spirit within you, and you shall live,"* and again, *"I will put my spirit within you, and make you follow my statutes and be careful to observe my ordinances"* (EZEKIEL 37:14; 36:27).

Blessed are we if we follow Mary's example in songs of praise.

O Mary,
thank you,
for you have sung and lived the Song of the Servant,
the hymn of joy,
in our name as well.
You have prayed for us
that we may join you in praise of God's greatness
and in the joy of being near to God.
And so we say, "thank you,"
together with all the saints
who in the new heaven and on the new earth
sing with you the praise of the Lord.

8. Jesus and Mary: Servants of God

"HE HAS LOOKED WITH FAVOR ON THE LOWLINESS OF HIS SERVANT. SURELY, FROM NOW ON ALL GENERATIONS WILL CALL ME BLESSED."

In the Magnificat, Mary shares with the Church her knowledge of the name of the Messiah, "the Servant of God," that the people of God may also come to know it ever more fully. She is worthy to sing the Song of the Servant, for she herself is totally a servant of God and humankind. In her life's song, Mary proclaims the name of Jesus and makes him known as the light for the nations and the salvation for all the earth.

What remains hidden to the wise and arrogant, God has revealed to his humble servant, Mary: the mystery of the kingdom that is proclaimed and brought into being by Jesus, the Servant. With great exultation, Jesus himself shares this truth with his disciples: *At that same hour Jesus rejoiced in the Holy Spirit and said, "I thank you, Father, Lord of heaven and earth, because you have hidden these things from the wise and the intelligent and have revealed them to infants; yes, Father, for such was your gracious will. All things have been handed over to me by my Father; and no one knows who the Son is except the Father, or who the Father is except the Son and anyone to whom the Son chooses to reveal him"* (LUKE 10:21-22).

We can assume that in this great moment Jesus was thinking of Mary, together with all who follow her in the path of humility. Nobody comes closer to the mystery of the Servant than Mary; for she knows that everything is a gift. Mary is blessed and worthy to be praised for she is a servant, immaculate, totally free from the stain of arrogance.Those who turn truly to Mary—and come to know her—will, with her, turn totally to Christ and will learn to know and to honor Jesus, the total Servant.

Mary is a spotless mirror, faithfully reflecting the grace of God.Therefore, we praise the Lord in calling her blessed among women. However, our praise is truly adoration of God if the humility of Mary, who follows Christ the Servant, becomes the program and purpose of our whole lives.When we truly come to know and to love Mary, we will ask her to pray that the same gift of humility may be granted to and received by us, so that the mystery of the kingdom of God can be revealed to us and through us.

Blessed are we if we follow Mary's example of humility.

O Mary,
we thank you for your song of humility and joy.
Pray for us
that we may fully be converted to Jesus Christ,
the Servant of God and Servant of humankind,
and thus be able to sing
with you
the song of joy before Jesus,
the Immanuel.

9. Mary's Vocation

"THE MIGHTY ONE HAS DONE GREAT THINGS FOR ME."

Sing for joy, O heavens, and exult, O earth; break forth, O mountains, into singing! For the LORD has comforted his people, and will have compassion on his suffering ones. Can a woman forget her nursing child, or show no compassion for the child of her womb? Even these may forget, yet I will not forget you. See, I have inscribed you on the palms of my hands; your walls are continually before me. Lift up your eyes all around and see; they all gather, they come to you. As I live, says the LORD, you shall put all of them on like an ornament, and like a bride you shall bind them on (ISAIAH 49:13,15-16,18).

In her boundless gratitude, Mary is able to discover God's wonderful works, done in and for her and for all of humanity. Only a lack of humility can prevent the discovery of all the wonderful things God has done.

Mary has received the greatest sign of love and the greatest vocation that could be bestowed upon a mere creature. She is full of grace, strong in faith, mother of the Lord. A new creation, she is the new Eve; through her, the new Adam comes to us. Mary is more than the first Eve, the mother of the living. God gathers the people around her, to make them all one family in Jesus Christ.

Through a profound love of Mary, who sings of her joy and gratitude throughout her whole life, we learn to have a memory filled with gratitude—to gain an awareness of all the wonderful gifts God has bestowed upon us. We discover our unique name, with which we are individually called by God. We come to a living faith in our vocation to holiness, a call to the ministry of unity and peace. When we gratefully discover the gifts of God in ourselves, we will be equally able to discover the inner resources of others. We will give credence and trust to our neighbor; and together we will become more conscious that the divine artist, the Holy Spirit, is present in our midst, forming us into masterpieces of God's love and wisdom.

To refuse to see the good that God has so wonderfully done in us is a great sin—against God, against self, against neighbor. From this blindness of an ungrateful people arises flight from responsibility and escape from reality—the sin of those who always live with "if only." Things are quite different when we learn to sing with Mary for joy and gratitude; in so doing, we also find courage and joy in responding to God's call: "Here am I, Lord. Call me, send me."

We and the world around us become much more human and blessed in learning to count the blessings of the Lord, in sharing in the praises of God's great goodness. We discover thousands of wonderful things, and waste much less time dwelling on existing evils.

Blessed are we if we follow Mary's example and count our blessings every day.

O Mary,
we thank you
for your life and your word
which teach us gratitude,
and help us to discover
all the wondrous things God has done for us
to the praise of God's holy Name,
and which prepare us to cooperate
with God's gracious calling.

10. Mary: Mother of Mercy

"HOLY IS HIS NAME. HIS MERCY IS FOR THOSE WHO FEAR HIM FROM GENERATION TO GENERATION."

I will take you for my wife forever; I will take you for my wife in righteousness and in justice, in steadfast love, and in mercy. I will take you for my wife in faithfulness; and you shall know the LORD (HOSEA 2:19-20).

In Mary, the new Eve, the Name of God is glorified in its holiness and mercy. Mary accepts all the songs of Israel in the name of the new Israel, the universal people of God chosen from all the nations. She also proclaims that God rejects the arrogant while always showing healing forgiveness and willing them to holiness. Mary sees God's promise fulfilled: *My heart recoils within me; my compassion grows warm and tender. I will not execute my fierce anger...for I am God and no mortal, the Holy One in your midst, and I will not come in wrath* (HOSEA 11:8B-9).

Mary's understanding of God is unforgettable. In the song of her life, there is a tension and harmony between holy fear before the all-holy God and total trust in God's compassionate love. Mary is herself a great sign of the mercy of God who, for the sake of Jesus, has protected her from all contamination with the patterns of evil embedded in the society of her day.

It is a sign of healthy religiosity that both fear and joyous trust are strong experiences in Mary's life. She is the model for all believers. The Church cannot be holy without constantly praising God's healing forgiveness and patience. Nor can the Church praise God's mercy without itself showing compassion toward sinners, the poor, the outcasts. No one is ever to be considered "hopeless," for fear of God's holy name prevents such rigorism. Those who sacrifice the person for the letter of the law, who show no compassion for people who find themselves in irregular situations, do not know the holy Name of God.

We are justified and sanctified by God's undeserved justice and mercy. The life and song of Mary are a commentary on the beatitude: *"Blessed are the merciful, for they will receive mercy"* (MATTHEW 5:7).

No one can live in this new justice without a readiness to follow Christ in his generosity and compassion. Jesus is honored with Mary when healing forgiveness is shown to friend and foe alike, when people act as channels of peace. Then all can praise the holy Name of God.

Blessed are we if we follow Mary's example of healing forgiveness toward all.

O Mary,
Mother of Perpetual Help,
your immaculate holiness and your absolute humility
are a great challenge
to turn away from all pride and self-centeredness,
and give the glory to God alone.
Thank you
for comforting us by your song of God's mercy,
daring us to go to the house of God
and say "Our Father...."
Pray for us, that all our life
may express childlike trust in the merciful Father of all.
Teach us that God is the holy One
and we, creatures and sinners,
can come to God only
because God's holiness is manifested through mercy.

11. Mary's Humility

"HE HAS SHOWN STRENGTH WITH HIS ARM; HE HAS SCATTERED THE PROUD IN THE THOUGHTS OF THEIR HEARTS. HE HAS BROUGHT DOWN THE POWERFUL FROM THEIR THRONES, AND LIFTED UP THE LOWLY."

Mary is inspired by the Old Testament's piety and profound vision of the history of salvation: *"As for me, I would seek God, and to God I would commit my cause. He does great things and unsearchable, marvelous things without number. He gives rain on the earth and sends waters on the fields; he sets on high those who are lowly, and those who mourn are lifted to safety. He frustrates the devices of the crafty, so that their hands achieve no success. He takes the wise in their own craftiness; and the schemes of the wily are brought to a quick end"* (JOB 5:8-13).

Our Lady of the Magnificat shows how false is an individualized religion. Mary is not in sympathy with those who think only of personal salvation and individual spiritual comfort. She is the companion of the Redeemer of the world. She discerns the profound meaning of the history of salvation. She sees the conflict between the Servant—who honors the all-holy, all-merciful God—and the dragon—the arrogant spirit that "proves" itself in overpowering people through misuse of authority and exploitation of the weak and the poor.

Mary knows the conflict between two different messianic expectations among the people of Israel. The priestly caste and the mighty of the land expect a powerful messiah, a national hero who can submit all other nations to the power of the Jews. Even some people of Nazareth, family members, and would-be disciples are captives of these false expectations. But Mary, from the very beginning, sings the true expectation: the Servant of God. The Messiah whom the Father sends will put the arrogant to rout. He opens the road of salvation to us by his humility, which is emulated by Mary, the humble deaconess who is to stand under his cross.

All of us should examine our own life history in light of the Magnificat, and especially, in light of the history of salvation in which Christ, the Servant, overcomes collective arrogance and pride. In this same perspective, the history of the Church should be studied. Visibly, the Church prospers and finds the assistance of God whenever it follows Christ, the Servant. Through a spirit of humility and gentleness, the Church can draw all people to Christ. If, with Mary, we sing the Song of the Servant, we will always better understand the profound meaning of the history of salvation. Before our eyes should always stand Jesus, who lived his daily life in humility. It is in the humble that Jesus continues to reveal himself.

Blessed are we if we follow Mary's example by humbly following Jesus, the Master of Humility.

O Mary,
how great are you,
how glorious,
how wonderful.
You have fully lived the mystery of salvation,
uncontaminated by a lust for power.
Pray for us,
that the Lord may keep us
far from the temptation to arrogance,
to vanity,
and to the exploitation of others.

12. Mary's Gratitude

"HE HAS FILLED THE HUNGRY WITH GOOD THINGS."

*Arise, shine; for your light has come, and the glory
of the LORD has risen upon you....Nations shall come
to your light, and kings to the brightness of your dawn.
Lift up your eyes and look around; they all gather
together, they come to you; your sons shall come from
far away, and your daughters shall be carried on their
nurses' arms.Then you shall see and be radiant; your
heart shall thrill and rejoice.... Your sun shall no more
go down, or your moon withdraw itself; for the LORD
will be your everlasting light, and your days of mourn-
ing shall be ended.Your people shall all be righteous....
The least of them shall become a clan, and the small-
est one a mighty nation; I am the LORD; in its time I
will accomplish it quickly* (ISAIAH 60:1,3-5A,20-21A,22).

Those who boast in their own power and cling to
their wealth cannot recognize the Servant of God, and
go empty-handed.Those who, in their arrogance, place
themselves above God cannot receive God's gifts. Only
those who honor God, and render thanks to God for
everything, receive grace. God responds to humankind's
hunger and thirst for justice and salvation, a hunger
which has been awakened by God's Spirit.

With all her being, Mary is the great teacher of the
gift of salvation. With Mary, we profess our faith: "We
believe in the Holy Spirit, the Lord, the giver of life."
God wants to share everything with us—supreme joy,
goodness, and wisdom. Mary praises God with her
whole life. Her spirit is filled with gratitude and she is
full of grace. In her humility and thankfulness, she is
the model of the Church whose mission, empowered

by the Holy Spirit, is to glorify God and help all people experience salvation.

We are called to nothing less than holiness. Through faith and baptism, we are a new creation. We can live united with Christ. But we must pray unceasingly that the Holy Spirit awaken in us an ever-increasing desire for the fullness of holiness—a desire to live with Mary in the discipleship of Christ's humility and purity of heart according to that undeserved gift of justification which we have received from God.

Before us stands Christ, who, infinitely rich, made himself poor so that in him we may be capable of sharing in the richness of God. Because he has humbled himself in his great hunger and thirst to make us rich, the Father has glorified him and given him "the name above all other names."

Blessed are we if we follow Mary's example and desire—with all our being—the fullness of holiness.

O Mary,
full of grace,
in your heart,
the hunger and thirst of Israel
—and of all of humankind—
for salvation
has come to fullness.
You,
who have experienced salvation,
pray for us,
that in humility, gratitude,
and hunger and thirst for God's saving justice,
we may prepare ourselves
for the much desired grace of a holy life.

13. Mary's Spirituality

"HE HAS HELPED HIS SERVANT ISRAEL, IN REMEMBRANCE OF HIS MERCY, ACCORDING TO THE PROMISE HE MADE TO OUR ANCESTORS, TO ABRAHAM AND TO HIS DESCENDANTS FOREVER."

With great intensity, Mary lives the history of salvation. She surely sang the great songs of the prophets long before she received the revelation that she was to be the virgin foretold by the prophets: *On that day this song will be sung in the land of Judah: We have a strong city; he sets up victory like walls and bulwarks. Open the gates, so that the righteous nation that keeps faith may enter in. Those of steadfast mind you keep in peace—in peace because they trust in you. Trust in the LORD forever, for in the LORD GOD you have an everlasting rock* (ISAIAH 26:1-4).

The Word that has taken human nature in Mary is the great sign of God's faithfulness and mercy. How could she not sing for joy and gratitude? In her, the great promises have been fulfilled! The One she bears is the new Israel, the Servant, the only begotten Son of God. From all corners of the earth, he will gather disciples who, with him and his mother, can sing in gratitude the song of the new Israel.

A key word of the Old Testament is *covenant*. The Magnificat shows us that the spirituality of Mary is covenant morality. She does not simply live as a private person. She lives before God, in full union with those who expected the Messiah before her and with those who in generations to come will praise the Lord with her. She teaches us how to celebrate and to live the Eucharist. She remembers gratefully all that God has done in the past, the promises God has made since the time of Abraham. In Mary, the history of Israel comes to full life as she anticipates the life of the new Israel, the Church. In Abraham, God has blessed his offspring. Blessed is Mary, and blessed is the fruit of her womb. Mary sings the song of Israel as the one who first experiences the fulfillment of the promises. Mary becomes the new model of faith for the new people of God.

After the words of the Magnificat, we read the prosaic note: *And Mary remained with her about three months and then returned to her home.*

The evangelist wants to remind us that Mary is in the house of Elizabeth to serve. She is, simultaneously, evangelist and handmaid. To this humble girl, God has opened the horizons of the history of salvation.

Blessed are we if we follow Mary's example of faithful obedience to the covenant.

O Mary,
we thank you for the Magnificat,
for the song of your life
which enchanted Elizabeth and Zechariah
and all who have met you.
We thank you
that in your life you have made visible
the mercy and fidelity of God,
who has done such great things in you.
Pray for us
that our gratitude may increase
and that we may evermore appreciate
the gifts of God
so that our life too may become a song
praising God's mercy and fidelity.

The Nativity

NOW THE BIRTH OF JESUS THE MESSIAH
TOOK PLACE IN THIS WAY.

When his mother Mary had been engaged to Joseph,
but before they lived together, she was found to be with
child from the Holy Spirit. Her husband Joseph, being a
righteous man and unwilling to expose her to public
disgrace, planned to dismiss her quietly. But just when
he had resolved to do this, an angel of the Lord appeared
to him in a dream and said, "Joseph, son of David, do not
be afraid to take Mary as your wife, for the child conceived in her is from the Holy Spirit. She will bear a son,
and you are to name him Jesus, for he will save his
people from their sins." All this took place to fulfill what
had been spoken by the Lord through the prophet:
"Look, the virgin shall conceive and bear a son, and they
shall name him Emmanuel," which means, "God is with
us."

When Joseph awoke from sleep, he did as the angel
of the Lord commanded him; he took her as his wife,
but had no marital relations with her until she had borne
a son; and he named him Jesus.

Matthew 1:18-25

IN THOSE DAYS a decree went out from Emperor Augustus that all the world should be registered. ...Joseph also went from the town of Nazareth in Galilee to Judea, to the city of David called Bethlehem, because he was descended from the house and family of David. He went to be registered with Mary....

While they were there, the time came for her to deliver her child. And she gave birth to her firstborn son and wrapped him in bands of cloth, and laid him in a manger, because there was no place for them in the inn.

In that region there were shepherds living in the fields, keeping watch over their flock by night. Then an angel of the Lord stood before them, and the glory of the Lord shone around them, and they were terrified. But the angel said to them, "Do not be afraid; for see— I am bringing you good news of great joy for all the people: to you is born this day in the city of David a Savior, who is the Messiah, the Lord. This will be a sign for you: you will find a child wrapped in bands of cloth and lying in a manger." And suddenly there was with the angel a multitude of the heavenly host, praising God and saying, "Glory to God in the highest heaven, and on earth peace among those whom he favors!"

When the angels had left them and gone into heaven...they went with haste and found Mary and Joseph, and the child lying in the manger. When they saw this, they made known what had been told them about this child; and all who heard it were amazed at what the shepherds told them. But Mary treasured all these words and pondered them in her heart. The shepherds returned, glorifying and praising God for all they had heard and seen, as it had been told them.

Luke 2:1-20

14. Mary and Joseph

"JOSEPH, SON OF DAVID, DO NOT BE AFRAID TO TAKE MARY AS YOUR WIFE, FOR THE CHILD CONCEIVED IN HER IS FROM THE HOLY SPIRIT. SHE WILL BEAR A SON, AND YOU ARE TO NAME HIM JESUS, FOR HE WILL SAVE HIS PEOPLE FROM THEIR SINS."

To see that the virgin betrothed to him is pregnant surely causes Joseph sleepless nights. Still, he does not allow himself to utter suspicion or accusation. Loving her, but feeling that he has no right to marry her, Joseph comes to a solution that can safeguard her reputation in a way that tradition cannot.

Joseph receives a revelation that opens up completely new horizons. He knows the Scriptures—that the virgin will give her son the name of Jesus. Now he is invited to share in the privilege of the virgin, to experience the nearness of God in Jesus, the Savior. Joseph is given to Mary and Jesus, as companion and support for the joyous days and for the crucial hours.

The history of the patriarchs, a history of faith and exodus, is lived again in Joseph. In him is made visible the history of the patriarchs at its best. Joseph accepts a mission into mystery, and he walks it in faith. At Mary's side, considered by law to be the father of Jesus, Joseph plays an active role in the history of salvation. In his humility and faith, he knows the name of Jesus: Emmanuel, "God-with-us." With Mary, he serenades Jesus with the Songs of the Servant by word and deed.

Arriving in Bethlehem, Joseph cannot find lodging for Mary to give birth in. Then, fleeing with his family, they live again the history of Israel as refugee people in Egypt. Finally returning to Nazareth, they put their trust in God alone. From a total lack of earthly security, the experience of God who is our rock comes to Joseph. He teaches us how to live in faith and hope with Mary and Jesus.

The Church of today lives anew that stunning exodus in the transition from one era to the next. We can look to the Holy Family, and learn that it is imperative for Christians to find strength in faith. The purpose of the Church's life to manifest trust in the Lord, to live in his presence and know that God will abide in us. The Lord alone is our stronghold.

Blessed are we if we look to Mary and Joseph for guidance and realize that our only strength is in God.

O Mary and Joseph,
we thank you
for having lived the moments of uncertainty and
  anguish
with purity of heart
and with one desire:
to be faithful to the Lord.
God's astounding plan
made you seek
new directions.
Though frustration was not spared you,
your faith
was only strengthened.
Protect us
by your intercession
that we may never forget
the presence of our Lord
who is our joy and our strength.

15. Mary's Firstborn

WHILE THEY WERE THERE, THE TIME CAME FOR HER TO DELIVER HER CHILD. AND SHE GAVE BIRTH TO HER FIRSTBORN SON AND WRAPPED HIM IN BANDS OF CLOTH, AND LAID HIM IN A MANGER, BECAUSE THERE WAS NO PLACE FOR THEM IN THE INN.

The great moment awaited by the whole world arrives. With the greatest intensity, Mary and Joseph live the exodus, the pilgrimage of Abraham and Isaac and Jacob, of the patriarch Joseph, of Moses, of the entire people of God. They anticipate the history of the pilgrim Church on earth.

In extreme poverty, but with faith and trust and a great love as their true riches, Mary and Joseph live this breathtaking moment in the history of salvation. The external circumstances of Christ's birth should not lead us to consider this child insignificant. This infant is everything in all things, the greatest gift of the Father to all creation. He is the child most wanted, most desired, most loved. He is Prince of Peace, King of kings.

This great moment reveals to us a true sense of poverty. Mary and Joseph tell us one great truth: God alone suffices. What more could they desire than to know him whom God has called and whom they will call Jesus, Savior, Emmanuel, God-with-us?

Jesus is called the firstborn of Mary. This does not mean that she gave birth to other children, but it does indicate that, in the "new" family of God, Jesus will have many brothers and sisters. He is the firstborn of all creation. In him—the eternal Word of the Father—are created all things, and all things have been made in view of him who came into the world as its light and life. He is the "only begotten Son," and yet the firstborn, for he calls us all to be his brothers and sisters, to join him in calling God "Abba, Father." It is in him that we can say, "Our Father." It is because of him that we have a right to call Mary our mother.

Blessed are we if we follow Mary's example and empty ourselves to be filled with a true sense of poverty.

O Mary,
how great must have been your joy
in that moment.
Pangs of childbirth,
the anguish of the exodus,
the poverty of the stall
are only the background of your joy.
You do not have any other treasure but Jesus,
your firstborn,
and you have no other desire
than to awaken our trust
in him who is Emmanuel,
God-with-us,
our salvation,
our joy.
Pray for us
that we may obtain that poverty of spirit
that allows us to find Jesus,
our only treasure,
our only love,
and to learn to love with him
all for whom he came
as Savior.
Pray for us
that we may put all our trust in him.

16. Mary: Mother of the Good Shepherd

**THEY WENT WITH HASTE AND FOUND MARY AND JO-
SEPH, AND THE CHILD LYING IN THE MANGER. WHEN
THEY SAW THIS, THEY MADE KNOWN WHAT HAD BEEN
TOLD THEM ABOUT THIS CHILD; AND ALL WHO HEARD
IT WERE AMAZED AT WHAT THE SHEPHERDS TOLD THEM.**

There is profound meaning in the fact that God revealed Jesus, the Son of Mary, first to the shepherds
through the song of the Messianic peace. This incident
calls to mind two of the great Messianic promises on
which Mary, and Joseph too, had meditated throughout
the years: that God would be the Good Shepherd; and
that God would both be Peace and bring to us the fullness of peace. *He will feed his flock like a shepherd; he
will gather the lambs in his arms, and carry them in
his bosom, and gently lead the mother sheep* (ISAIAH
40:11). *I myself will be the shepherd of my sheep, and
I will make them lie down, says the Lord GOD. I will
seek the lost, and I will bring back the strayed, and I
will bind up the injured, and I will strengthen the
weak, but the fat and the strong I will destroy. I will
feed them with justice* (EZEKIEL 34:15-16).

Mary knows that Jesus has not come to judge or to
condemn, but rather to seek out and heal the lost. When
we see through the eyes of Mary and the Christmas
shepherds, we too find Jesus, and we rejoice with the
angels.

Mary treasures in her heart the message brought by
the shepherds and the angels. Her meditation on Jesus,
Prince of Peace and Good Shepherd, includes us: that
the Church may never lack good shepherds shaped in
the image of Christ, nor be without those who rejoice

in the peace of Christ and share it with all people. When we celebrate these great events in the Eucharist, we remember Mary with gratitude, thankful for the message that is brought to us in order that we be fully open to the grace and joy of the Good News. A genuine veneration of Mary leads us to understand the Eucharist more fully. It transforms all our life into a Magnificat.

Blessed are we if we see through the eyes of Mary and understand the Eucharist more fully.

O Mary,
mother of the Good Shepherd,
pray for us
and pray for the shepherds of the Church
that they may truly and fully know
the name of Jesus,
the Good Shepherd.
Pray that their hearts,
filled with compassionate mercy for those who have
 gone astray,
may patiently seek them out
and gently bring them home
into their Father's house.
Pray for us
that gratitude
may inspire all our thoughts,
all our desires,
all our deeds.

The
Presentation

AFTER EIGHT DAYS HAD PASSED,
it was time to circumcise the child; and he was called
Jesus, the name given by the angel before he was conceived in the womb. When the time came for their
purification according to the law of Moses, they brought
him up to Jerusalem to present him to the Lord....

Now there was a man in Jerusalem whose name was
Simeon; this man was righteous and devout...and the
Holy Spirit rested on him. It had been revealed to him
by the Holy Spirit that he would not see death before
he had seen the Lord's Messiah. Guided by the Spirit,
Simeon came into the temple; and when the parents
brought in the child Jesus,...Simeon took him in his
arms and praised God, saying, "Master, now you are dis-
missing your servant in peace, according to your word;
for my eyes have seen your salvation, which you have
prepared in the presence of all peoples, a light for revelation to the Gentiles and for glory to your people
Israel."...Then Simeon blessed them and said to his
mother Mary, "This child is destined for the falling and
the rising of many in Israel, and to be a sign that will be
opposed so that the inner thoughts of many will be revealed—and a sword will pierce your own soul too...."

When they had finished everything required by the
law of the Lord, they returned to Galilee, to their own
town of Nazareth. The child grew and became strong,
filled with wisdom; and the favor of God was upon him.

Luke 2:21-40

17. Mary and the Covenant

**AFTER EIGHT DAYS HAD PASSED, IT WAS TIME TO CIR-
CUMCISE THE CHILD; AND HE WAS CALLED JESUS, THE
NAME GIVEN BY THE ANGEL BEFORE HE WAS CONCEIVED
IN THE WOMB.**

When Jesus is presented for circumcision, his name
is solemnly proclaimed: Jesus, "God our Savior." The
covenant of God with Abraham and Moses is proclaimed
in this one who is "the covenant of the people." *This is
my covenant, which you shall keep, between me and
you and your offspring after you: Every male among
you shall be circumcised.... Throughout your generations every male among you shall be circumcised
when he is eight days old* (GENESIS 17:10,12A).

The ritual of circumcision is a profound renewal of
the commitment to the covenant and the law of the
covenant: to love God with all our hearts, with all our
souls, and with all our energies, and to love our neighbor as ourselves. Jesus' circumcision marks the fulfillment of the covenant God promised to Abraham and
his descendants, for with the coming of Jesus the new
covenant begins. *I am the LORD, I have called you in
righteousness, I have taken you by the hand and kept
you; I have given you as a covenant to the people, a
light to the nations* (ISAIAH 42:6).

Jesus is our incarnate source of unity. He establishes
the law of saving solidarity, mutual active dependence
and love for all. Jesus' personal manifestation of the new
covenant is solemnly marked with his baptism in the
Jordan. His appearance there and his desire for baptism
indicate that he is ready to bear the burdens of all
peoples. With his public commitment, the Holy Spirit

comes visibly upon him and the Father proclaims him as his beloved Son.

In baptism, we solemnly receive the honor and the name of children of God. For us, the name of Jesus is always a prayer of praise and of petition. We place our trust in him, and we bless each other in his holy Name. Jesus' circumcision and the baptism are liturgical preparations for that great moment when Jesus receives the real baptism in his blood, which is and will always be the blood of the new and everlasting covenant.

Blessed are we as we receive the honor and the name of children of God.

O Mary,
how great must have been your joy
when, at the circumcision,
you could proclaim the name of Jesus,
whom you recognized
as "the covenant of the people."
Pray for us
that we may better understand
the meaning of the new and everlasting covenant
and thus come to live fully,
in communal love,
our birthright
which baptism has given us.

18. Jesus Is Presented

WHEN THE TIME CAME FOR THEIR PURIFICATION AC-CORDING TO THE LAW OF MOSES, THEY BROUGHT HIM UP TO JERUSALEM TO PRESENT HIM TO THE LORD.

The presentation of Jesus in the Temple is, like the circumcision, an act of obedience to the law of the old covenant. Thus it is a prophetic gesture that announces the coming of the new covenant—that of the anointed one, Christ, the High Priest and Prophet.

Through Moses, God has explained the profound meaning of this act of presentation: *"Consecrate to me all the firstborn; whatever is the first to open the womb among the Israelites, of human beings and animals, is mine.... When the LORD has brought you into the land of the Canaanites, as he swore to you and your ancestors, and has given it to you.... you shall set apart to the LORD all that first opens the womb.... When in the future your child asks you, 'What does this mean?' you shall answer, 'By strength of hand the LORD brought us out of Egypt, from the house of slavery'"* (EXODUS 13:2,11-12A,14).

Mary, in obedience to the law, fulfills this ritual praising God for the liberation from the bondage of slavery. She knows that Jesus belongs to God the Father in a unique way. The ritual is only a manifestation of the deepest truth: that Jesus, from the beginning, is totally consecrated to the kingdom of the Father and to the Gospel. But it becomes gradually clear to Mary that this road of Jesus' will require detachment and great sacrifice on her part. At the proper moment, she will humbly hide herself, as John the Baptist will also do, so that

Jesus, in his uniqueness, may be manifested to all as the Prophet, the Priest, and the Sacrifice.

The presentation of the firstborn is an act of consecration. As Mary fulfills this act, presenting the child who is consecrated by the Holy Spirit, she consecrates herself as his companion and servant. She knows that the ritual sacrifice of a pair of turtledoves cannot substitute for the offering of herself. This is so, especially in view of Christ who comes to offer himself.

At the baptism of Jesus in the Jordan, the dove becomes the symbol of the consecration through the Holy Spirit. Mary, with dove-like simplicity, is always faithful and docile to the promptings of the Holy Spirit, and thus fulfills her role in the work of redemption. Through the gifts of the Holy Spirit, she perceives what the Lord asks of her, as she offers her firstborn in the Temple and at every stage of her life.

Blessed are we if, like Mary, we are always faithful and docile to the promptings of the Holy Spirit.

O Mary,
present us
with Jesus
to the Father in heaven.
Pray for us
that we may learn
what a great joy it is
to know that we belong to God,
are consecrated to God,
together with your firstborn,
Jesus Christ.

19. Mary: Queen of the Prophets

THEN SIMEON BLESSED THEM AND SAID TO HIS MOTHER
MARY, "THIS CHILD IS DESTINED FOR THE FALLING AND
THE RISING OF MANY IN ISRAEL."...AT THAT MOMENT
[ANNA] CAME, AND BEGAN TO PRAISE GOD AND TO
SPEAK ABOUT THE CHILD TO ALL WHO WERE LOOKING
FOR THE REDEMPTION OF JERUSALEM.

The Gospel of Luke presents Mary very clearly to us
as the queen of the prophets. When she brings her greeting and blessing to the house of Zechariah, John, still in
the womb, leaps for joy, thus initiating his prophetic
role of proclaiming the One who would baptize by the
Holy Spirit. Elizabeth is filled with the Holy Spirit and,
after a period of silence, Zechariah utters the great
prophecy in a song similar to Mary's own.

When Mary presents Jesus in the Temple, another
astonishing encounter with the prophets takes place.
Two other noble representatives of the humble people of
Israel encounter him. The outpouring of the Holy Spirit
upon Elizabeth and Zechariah and upon Simeon and
Anna is a sign of the new messianic era. It becomes clear
that God reveals God's self to the humble and the simple.

Simeon and Anna are privileged ones to whom God
reveals the coming of the Messiah. The encounter is an
occasion for the praise of the Lord, and the revelation
granted to this holy group becomes, at once, proclama-
tion of the things to come. Mary receives these prophetic voices of joyous praise and evangelization as the
queen of the evangelists and apostles. How she longs
that all people may know the Savior!

Mary too receives a special prophecy, that of the
sword of suffering. She is the one who is to follow Christ

wherever he goes, even to the abyss of suffering. From now on, the participation of Mary in the mystery of salvation comes to fuller light. Mary shares in Christ's suffering. Because of her great love, her immaculate heart will suffer more than any other. It is from Christ, however, that her share in the work of redemption has its great fecundity.

Faced with Jesus Christ, all of us have to make a decision for or against him. The greatest pain for Jesus is to see that some resist, and refuse salvation. This also is the sharpest sword that wounds the heart of Mary since, through her son, the Son of God, she is mother of all the living. As such, she desires nothing more than the salvation of all people.

Blessed are we if, like Mary, all our decisions are for Jesus.

O Mary,
we honor you
as queen of the prophets.
Pray for us
that we may always be open
to the grace
of the Holy Spirit
and to the voices
of those who call us to total conversion.

The Epiphany

IN THE TIME OF KING HEROD, after Jesus was born in Bethlehem of Judea, wise men from the East came to Jerusalem, asking, "Where is the child who has been born king of the Jews? For we observed his star at its rising, and have come to pay him homage." When King Herod heard this, he was frightened, and all Jerusalem with him; and calling together all the chief priests and scribes of the people, he inquired of them where the Messiah was to be born. They told him, "In Bethlehem of Judea; for so it has been written by the prophet: 'And you, Bethlehem, in the land of Judah, are by no means least among the rulers of Judah; for from you shall come a ruler who is to shepherd my people Israel.'" Then Herod secretly called for the wise men and learned from them the exact time when the star had appeared. Then he sent them to Bethlehem, saying, "Go and search diligently for the child; and when you have found him, bring me word so that I may also go and pay him homage."

When they had heard the king, they set out; and there, ahead of them, went the star that they had seen at its rising, until it stopped over the place where the child was. ... On entering the house, they saw the child with Mary his mother; and they knelt down and paid him homage. Then, opening their treasure chests, they offered him gifts of gold, frankincense, and myrrh. And having been warned in a dream not to return to Herod, they left for their own country by another road.

Now after they had left, an angel of the Lord appeared to Joseph in a dream and said, "Get up, take the child and his mother, and flee to Egypt, and remain there until I tell you; for Herod is about to search for the child, to destroy him." Then Joseph got up, took the child and his mother by night, and went to Egypt, and remained there until the death of Herod. This was to fulfill what had been spoken by the Lord through the prophet, "Out of Egypt I have called my son."

When Herod saw that he had been tricked by the wise men, he was infuriated, and he sent and killed all the children in and around Bethlehem who were two years old or under, according to the time that he had learned from the wise men. Then was fulfilled what had been spoken through the prophet Jeremiah: "A voice was heard in Ramah, wailing and loud lamentation, Rachel weeping for her children; she refused to be consoled, because they are no more."

When Herod died, an angel of the Lord suddenly appeared in a dream to Joseph in Egypt and said, "Get up, take the child and his mother, and go to the land of Israel, for those who were seeking the child's life are dead." Then Joseph got up, took the child and his mother, and went to the land of Israel. But when he heard that Archelaus was ruling over Judea in place of his father Herod, he was afraid to go there.

And after being warned in a dream, he went away to the district of Galilee. There he made his home in a town called Nazareth, so that what had been spoken through the prophets might be fulfilled, "He will be called a Nazorean."

Matthew 2:1-23

20. Mary and the Magi

ON ENTERING THE HOUSE, THEY SAW THE CHILD WITH MARY HIS MOTHER; AND THEY KNELT DOWN AND PAID HIM HOMAGE.

The visit of the Magi presents a profound vision about Jesus, light of all nations, center and summit of all history. Joyous, Mary realizes the first fulfillment of the prophecy of Simeon: that her son is the light of all nations. Again, we see the relatedness of Mary to the evangelization of all the world.

The Epiphany event proclaims a joyful fulfillment of the prophecy of Isaiah: *Then you shall see and be radiant; your heart shall thrill and rejoice, because the abundance of the sea shall be brought to you, the wealth of the nations shall come to you. A multitude of camels shall cover you, the young camels of Midian and Ephah; all those from Sheba shall come. They shall bring gold and frankincense, and shall proclaim the praise of the LORD* (ISAIAH 60:5-6).

Mary rejoices in all who give themselves to Jesus in the purity of their heart, symbolized by the gift of gold. The purity of motives with which so many seek and find the Lord is related to the immaculate heart of Mary who serves God with the purity of her entire being. Her heart overflows with joy when she sees the multitudes who seek and find her son because of the purity of their motives.

The Magi offer the gift of frankincense, the symbol of adoration. Mary leads the choir of all who praise and adore the Lord in all their lives. If we come to Mary, we can learn from her how to follow Christ as true adorers of the Father.

The Magi offer the gift of myrrh, which reminds us of the death and sepulchre of Christ. Later, when Mary of Bethany anoints the feet of Jesus with a pound of a very costly perfume, Jesus spells out the meaning of what she does: *"Leave her alone. She bought it so that she might keep it for the day of my burial"* (JOHN 12:7).

Mary, the mother of Jesus, is closest to Jesus beneath the cross, and at the sepulchre where he was buried. Her presence there is the final test of her adoration of God in truth and fullness, which comes from the Holy Spirit.

Blessed are we if, like Mary, we follow Christ as true adorers of the Father.

O Mary,
you have offered yourself
to God
as pure gold.
Seeing your joy at the Epiphany,
we ask you to pray for us
that we might consider it the greatest privilege
to be sent as messengers of the Good News
and to preach the Gospel,
whatever may be the cost.

21. Holy Family in Exile

"GET UP, TAKE THE CHILD AND HIS MOTHER, AND FLEE TO EGYPT."

Mary and Joseph escape into Egypt to save the life of the child. In the land of exile, the prophecy of Simeon comes true. A special divine providence protects the child and his mother, and Joseph is chosen to be the visible sign of this protection.

The Holy Family relives the history of salvation, a history of exodus and liberation. Joseph the patriarch was sold by his brothers and brought as a slave to Egypt to become savior to his brothers. Jacob had to go to Egypt, and Moses and the people suffered there under fierce oppression until the Lord freed them from the land of slavery.

In the liberation of Israel, God acts as Father: *When Israel was a child, I loved him, and out of Egypt I called my son* (HOSEA 11:1). This comes to full truth in Jesus, who has to escape to Egypt and experience the saving action of the Father. He is the "beloved Son," and yet he suffers with the downtrodden, with the homeless, with the persecuted.

We have seen millions of people, all over the world, who have been driven out of their homeland. Many are migrants, looking for work and a piece of bread. No book can ever contain all the misery and humiliation endured by many. Yet, Jesus has taken upon himself this painful exodus, so others should not consider theirs to be meaningless. We honor the Holy Family who escaped into Egypt when we sympathize with today's homeless and oppressed peoples.

When they return to the land of Galilee, surely the

Holy Family learn of the "slaughter of the innocents" and other crimes of Herod. Imagine the greatness of Mary's compassion, the suffering of her immaculate heart upon hearing this. Indeed, the prophecy of Simeon stayed with her always.

Blessed are we if we follow Mary's example of compassion to others, especially innocent victims of abuse and crime.

O Mary,
we pray to you,
our mother of perpetual help.
May all believers
learn from your generosity;
may all rulers of countries
honor God,
the one Father,
by a greater concern
for those
who are rejected, lonely, homeless.
Pray for us
that we may learn compassion,
and unite our actions
in favor of those who are most in need.

Jesus' "Hidden Life"

NOW EVERY YEAR his parents went to Jerusalem for the festival of the Passover. And when he was twelve years old, they went up as usual for the festival. When the festival was ended and they started to return, the boy Jesus stayed behind in Jerusalem, but his parents did not know it. Assuming that he was in the group of travelers, they went a day's journey. Then they started to look for him among their relatives and friends. When they did not find him, they returned to Jerusalem to search for him.

After three days they found him in the temple, sitting among the teachers, listening to them and asking them questions. And all who heard him were amazed at his understanding and his answers.

When his parents saw him they were astonished; and his mother said to him, "Child, why have you treated us like this? Look, your father and I have been searching for you in great anxiety." He said to them, "Why were you searching for me? Did you not know that I must be in my Father's house?" But they did not understand what he said to them.

Then he went down with them and came to Nazareth, and was obedient to them. His mother treasured all these things in her heart. And Jesus increased in wisdom and in years, and in divine and human favor.

Luke 2:41-52

22. Jesus in the Temple

"WHY WERE YOU SEARCHING FOR ME? DID YOU NOT KNOW THAT I MUST BE IN MY FATHER'S HOUSE?"

The event in the Temple foreshadows the time when Jesus will leave his home in Nazareth to spend forty days in the desert, later to become a pilgrim in Galilee and Judea. The three days, filled with anguish for Mary and Joseph, give a glimpse of the future, to those three dark days between Jesus' death and Resurrection.

This is the first time we hear Jesus call God, "my Father." These words point to his "new family," the whole family of the redeemed that is based upon the unique relationship of Jesus of Nazareth to the Fatherhood of God.

Mary is called to enter into a deeper awareness: She is to be the mother of the Church. Hers is a motherhood in the new family of God, based on the relationship of Jesus to his heavenly Father and the Holy Spirit. She is not able to at once understand the full depth of the events or the words of Jesus, but she treasures his words in her heart until she comes to a full understanding. In Jesus and in Mary there is no shadow of sin, but they too live under the law of growth. Luke, twice in one chapter, emphasizes that *Jesus increases in wisdom and in years, and in divine and human favor* (2:40,52). This is important for the Church, as we gradually grasp our mission and continue to interpret the signs of the times.

The new family of God manifests itself everywhere, throughout history, where people are moved by the Spirit of God and recognize themselves as sons and daughters of God. *For you did not receive a spirit of slavery to fall back into fear, but you have received a spirit of adoption. When we cry, "Abba! Father!" it is that very Spirit bearing witness with our spirit that we are children of God* (ROMANS 8:15-16).

Blessed are we if, like the child Jesus and his mother Mary, we continue to grow in our awareness and understanding of God.

O Mary,
we thank you
for your motherly care of Jesus,
our brother and our Lord.
We are deeply touched
by your pain and anguish
in that prophetic event
foreshadowing
three even more anguishing days
after the death of your son,
Jesus Christ.
Pray for us
that we may treasure the words of Jesus
in our hearts
as you did
and that we may be patient and faithful
in our common effort
to reach a deeper understanding
of the words of Jesus
and a fuller discernment
of the signs of the times.

The Wedding Feast

ON THE THIRD DAY

there was a wedding in Cana of Galilee, and the mother of Jesus was there. Jesus and his disciples had also been invited to the wedding.

When the wine gave out, the mother of Jesus said to him, "They have no wine." And Jesus said to her, "Woman, what concern is that to you and to me? My hour has not yet come." His mother said to the servants, "Do whatever he tells you."

Now standing there were six stone water jars for the Jewish rites of purification, each holding twenty or thirty gallons. Jesus said to them, "Fill the jars with water." And they filled them up to the brim. He said to them, "Now draw some out, and take it to the chief steward." So they took it.

When the steward tasted the water that had become wine, and did not know where it came from (though the servants who had drawn the water knew), the steward called the bridegroom and said to him, "Everyone serves the good wine first, and then the inferior wine after the guests have become drunk. But you have kept the good wine until now."

Jesus did this, the first of his signs, in Cana of Galilee, and revealed his glory; and his disciples believed in him.

After this he went down to Capernaum with his mother, his brothers, and his disciples; and they remained there a few days.

John 2:1-12

23. Mary at Cana

HIS MOTHER SAID TO THE SERVANTS, "DO WHATEVER HE TELLS YOU."

This narrative is, at the same time, a manifestation of Mary's loving attention to the earthly needs of people and of her prophetic intuition. Again we find her in Cana as a humble servant who helps out in the household. It is perhaps a gesture of courtesy toward Mary that Jesus and his disciples are invited. The wine runs out, and she brings the matter before her son. She does not tell Jesus what to do. Her prayer is courageous, and at the same time humble.

Jesus' miracle at Cana, in response to his mother, is a prophetic event, rich in meaning and opening up new horizons. Mary's words to the servants deserve our special attention: *"Do whatever he tells you."* This is at the heart of true Marian devotion. We honor her as we follow him and do whatever he tells us.

Jesus addresses his mother as "Woman," the same expression used by God in the Garden of Eden: *"I will put enmity between you and the woman"* (GENESIS 3:15). From the cross, Jesus again addresses his mother as "Woman" (JOHN 19:26). The vision of the great woman found in the Bible's first book comes to full magnitude in its final book (REVELATION, chapter 12). In the eyes of Jesus, in that solemn moment at Cana, Mary is more than his "private" mother. She is the great sign of promise, a prophetic sign affirmed by the first miracle which Jesus works in view of her, the "Woman."

Jesus says, *"My hour has not yet come."* The present event, notable as it is, has to be read in light of the "exalted" hour, when Jesus is to shed the blood of the

new and eternal covenant in a wedding of himself—
forever—with redeemed humanity. Christ is the spouse
who preserves the best wine until the end.

The embarrassment of the spouses at Cana, which
gives rise to such a great miracle, is a modest symbol of
the profound suffering in which the wedding between
Christ and the Church is rehearsed. Mary is present to
both events. She will always invite and urge us: *"Do
whatever he tells you."* Her words are both exhortation
and gift.

Blessed are we if we listen to Mary and do whatever
Jesus tells us.

O Mary,
how beautiful is your trusting prayer!
You know
how to honor Jesus
by your prayer.
Pray for us
that we,
like you at Cana,
may learn to intercede for each other,
being always ready
to bear each other's burdens.

Hometown Rejection

HE STOOD UP TO READ,
and the scroll of the prophet Isaiah was given to him.
He unrolled the scroll and found the place where it was
written: "The Spirit of the Lord is upon me, because he
has anointed me to bring good news to the poor. He has
sent me to proclaim release to the captives and recovery
of sight to the blind, to let the oppressed go free, to proclaim the year of the Lord's favor." And he rolled up the
scroll, gave it back to the attendant, and sat down.

The eyes of all in the synagogue were fixed on him.
Then he began to say to them, "Today this scripture has
been fulfilled in your hearing." All spoke well of him
and were amazed at the gracious words that came from
his mouth. They said, "Is not this Joseph's son?"

He said to them, "Doubtless you will quote to me
this proverb, 'Doctor, cure yourself!' And you will say,
'Do here also in your hometown the things that we
have heard you did at Capernaum.'" And he said, "Truly
I tell you, no prophet is accepted in the prophet's hometown. But the truth is, there were many widows in Israel in the time of Elijah…yet Elijah was sent to none of
them except to a widow at Zarephath in Sidon."

When they heard this, all in the synagogue were filled
with rage. They got up, drove him out of the town, and
led him to the brow of the hill…so that they might hurl
him off the cliff. But he passed through the midst of
them and went on his way.

Luke 4:13-30

THEN HE WENT HOME;

and the crowd came together again, so that they could not even eat. When his family heard it, they went out to restrain him, for people were saying, "He has gone out of his mind." And the scribes who came down from Jerusalem said, "He has Beelzebul, and by the ruler of the demons he casts out demons." And he called them to him, and spoke to them in parables, "How can Satan cast out Satan? If a kingdom is divided against itself, that kingdom cannot stand. And if a house is divided against itself, that house will not be able to stand. And if Satan has risen up against himself and is divided, he cannot stand, but his end has come. But no one can enter a strong man's house and plunder his property without first tying up the strong man; then indeed the house can be plundered.

"Truly I tell you, people will be forgiven for their sins and whatever blasphemies they utter; but whoever blasphemes against the Holy Spirit can never have forgiveness, but is guilty of an eternal sin"—for they had said, "He has an unclean spirit."

Then his mother and his brothers came; and standing outside, they sent to him and called him. A crowd was sitting around him; and they said to him, "Your mother and your brothers and sisters are outside, asking for you." And he replied, "Who are my mother and my brothers?" And looking at those who sat around him, he said, "Here are my mother and my brothers! Whoever does the will of God is my brother and sister and mother."

Mark 3:19b-35

24. Rejection in Nazareth

**AND HE SAID, "TRULY I TELL YOU, NO PROPHET IS AC-
CEPTED IN THE PROPHET'S HOMETOWN...."**

The heart of the prophet Isaiah must have been pierced when the Lord bade him to announce this terrible suffering of God's own heart: *Hear, O heavens, and listen, O earth; for the LORD has spoken: I reared children and brought them up, but they have rebelled against me. The ox knows its owner, and the donkey its master's crib; but Israel does not know, my people do not understand* (ISAIAH 1:2-3). So too does Mary's heart ache when she experiences the fulfillment of this prophecy in her hometown of Nazareth.

Why is Jesus rejected by his own townsfolk? Jesus comes from humble people. Everyone knows his mother, and that the family lives in lowly social conditions. Under these circumstances, Jesus presents himself explicitly as the Servant of God and of the people. His origins and family lifestyle refute false messianic expectations. Many anticipate a national hero. Besides, as the gospel text indicates, hometowners want a miracle worker for their own greater glory. They are jealous because he now makes his home in Capernaum, and works great "signs" of healing there. The townspeople believe he is sinning against their collective interests.

This conduct of the people of Nazareth symbolically expresses the sin of a great part of Israel. The high priest, the Pharisees, the powerful, look upon religion as a means. Because Jesus refuses to play into the hands of such people, he is rejected and scorned. This sad event in Nazareth is a prophecy of what will happen on Calvary.

We see Mary as one who suffers, in this moment and throughout the coming years, for all the sins of human-kind. This serves as a motive to venerate Mary, who teaches us how to follow Jesus in humility and detachment, sharing in Christ's suffering. Honoring Mary means never using the Church for personal gain, prestige, wealth, or power. Rather, it means honoring the Church as humble servants of Christ.

Blessed are we if we learn from Mary how to follow Jesus in both humility and detachment.

O Mary,
we honor your suffering,
your pain
caused by those whom you loved.
How deep
must have been the wound in your heart
when you saw Jesus rejected by your neighbors!
We are all written into your heart
and we should know
how deeply we wound your heart
when we refuse
to accept Christ as the Servant
and follow him in humility as you did.
Pray for us
that we may come to accept
all the frustrations and sufferings
with which the Lord allows us to be afflicted
on this road of salvation,
and thus come to know more intensely,
Christ, the Suffering Servant,
and you, our mother,
who followed him on his road.

25. Mary and the Will of God

**"WHOEVER DOES THE WILL OF GOD IS MY BROTHER
AND SISTER AND MOTHER."**

It becomes increasingly clear that Jesus has not come
to build up his own little family, but rather to bring into
being a worldwide family of disciples, a family based
entirely upon the universal Fatherhood of God, his
Father, with he himself as brother of all.

From this perspective, we can understand our own
family, particularly when the family tries to obstruct our
total adherence to the kingdom of God. Detachment is
one aspect, a part of the wonderful expression of the
Good News that those who follow Christ wholeheartedly, whatever the price, are as dear to him as brothers
and sisters are; even as dear to him as his mother is. *"As
the Father has loved me, so I have loved you"* (JOHN
15:9).

Jesus' response to those who did not yet know that
he was the cornerstone of a new universal family does
not at all estrange us from Mary. Rather, it helps us to
understand her role in the new family of God. And
we know that she will be present to us in our moments
of severest temptation if only we are ready to follow
the Servant of God.

Mary, totally consecrated to the kingdom of the
Father and to the mission of the Servant of God, is never
an obstacle to the mission of Christ. On the contrary,
her entire life helps us to understand the meaning of
detachment, of exodus, as she follows Christ in his most
crucial moments. If we are ready to follow Mary along
this road, in our moments of deepest suffering we will
more fully understand what it means to be as dear to

Jesus as his mother is. We will hear and understand the words: *[Jesus] said to [his] disciple, "Here is your mother"* (JOHN 19:27).

Blessed are we if we understand what it means to be as dear to Jesus as his mother is.

O Mary,
in the midst of the pain
caused by members of your family,
you rejoiced,
assured by your son that he loves all of us,
your children,
with the same love with which he loves you.
Knowing this,
we also know
how great your love is for us
when we put all our trust in Jesus.
Pray for us
that we may be grateful for this privilege
and that nothing in this world
will hinder us
from following Christ wholeheartedly
as members of the new family
which honors the one Father in heaven
and pays tribute also to you,
the mother of the living.

Active Ministry

NOW HE WAS CASTING OUT a demon that was mute; when the demon had gone out, the one who had been mute spoke, and the crowds were amazed. But some of them said, "He casts out demons by Beelzebul, the ruler of the demons." Others, to test him, kept demanding from him a sign from heaven.

But he knew what they were thinking and said to them, "Every kingdom divided against itself becomes a desert, and house falls on house. If Satan also is divided against himself, how will his kingdom stand?—for you say that I cast out the demons by Beelzebul. Now if I cast out the demons by Beelzebul, by whom do your exorcists cast them out? Therefore they will be your judges. But if it is by the finger of God that I cast out the demons, then the kingdom of God has come to you.…Whoever is not with me is against me, and whoever does not gather with me scatters.

While he was saying this, a woman in the crowd raised her voice and said to him, "Blessed is the womb that bore you and the breasts that nursed you!" But he said, "Blessed rather are those who hear the word of God and obey it!"

Luke 11:14-28

26. Mary: Model for Good Listeners

BUT HE SAID, "BLESSED RATHER ARE THOSE WHO HEAR
THE WORD OF GOD AND OBEY IT!"

A humble woman in the crowd, with great admiration and faith, praises Jesus by praising his mother. Jesus accepts this beautiful expression of human sentiment but, as always, gives it a deeper meaning. Not wanting to diminish the glory of his mother, he emphasizes the one dimension that is the true glory of Mary: She is the mother in the new family of God whose openness to the Word of God is dedicated to living the truth.

In the Sermon on the Mount, Jesus most solemnly teaches that it is not sufficient to simply call oneself his disciple. What is needed is openness to his Word as a listener and a responder: *"Not everyone who says to me, 'Lord, Lord,' will enter the kingdom of heaven, but only the one who does the will of my Father in heaven....Everyone then who hears these words of mine and acts on them will be like a wise man who built his house on rock"* (MATTHEW 7:21,24). Thus is revealed to us the true motherhood of Mary as the model of the Church: She lives by every word that comes from the mouth of God and is totally dedicated to act upon that word.

The future of Christianity depends greatly upon each community knowing how to celebrate the Eucharist, the memorial of our Lord's suffering, death, and Resurrection, which means also being prepared to live according to this mystery. Mary is the perfect eucharistic person: one who remembers with perfect gratitude and who inspires fidelity in our commitment to the kingdom of God.

If we want to be authentic members of this new family, grounded on faith in Christ, we have to learn more deeply the art of discovering the signs of God's presence. We must listen to God's Word everywhere: in all of creation; in all people as image and likeness of God; in the saints and the prophets; and in the wonderful message of the sacraments. And we must always rely on the grace of the Holy Spirit to help us discover the message and the will of God. We should daily meditate upon the Holy Scriptures, and we should give full attention to the teaching authority of the Church, in order to better understand the total message of Christ. But the heart of the matter is always what Mary teaches us: *"Do whatever he tells you."*

Blessed are we if we, like Mary, listen to God's Word everywhere.

O Mary,
pray for us
that the Lord may give to us,
as he gave to you,
a memory filled with gratitude,
so that each day
we may learn
how to celebrate the Eucharist properly,
and live our life
in grateful response to all of God's gifts.

The Crucifixion

NOW IT WAS THE DAY of Preparation for the Passover; and it was about noon. He said to the Jews, "Here is your King!" They cried out, "Away with him! Away with him! Crucify him!" Pilate asked them, "Shall I crucify your King?" The chief priests answered, "We have no king but the emperor." Then he handed him over to them to be crucified. So they took Jesus; and carrying the cross by himself, he went out to…Golgotha. There they crucified him, and with him two others.…

Pilate also had an inscription written and put on the cross. It read, "Jesus of Nazareth, the King of the Jews".… Then the chief priests…said to Pilate, "Do not write, 'The King of the Jews,' but, 'This man said, I am King of the Jews.'" Pilate answered, "What I have written I have written."

Meanwhile, standing near the cross of Jesus were his mother, and his mother's sister, Mary the wife of Clopas, and Mary Magdalene…Jesus…said to his mother, "Woman, here is your son." Then he said to the disciple, "Here is your mother." And from that hour the disciple took her into his own home.

After this, when Jesus knew that all was now finished, he said…, "I am thirsty." A jar full of sour wine was standing there. So they put a sponge full of the wine on a branch of hyssop and held it to his mouth. When Jesus had received the wine, he said, "It is finished." Then he bowed his head and gave up his spirit.

John 19:14-30

THEN THEY LED HIM AWAY

to crucify him. As they went out, they came upon a man from Cyrene named Simon; they compelled this man to carry his cross....

And when they had crucified him, they divided his clothes among themselves by casting lots; then they sat down there and kept watch over him. Over his head they put the charge against him, which read, "This is Jesus, the King of the Jews." Then two bandits were crucified with him, one on his right and one on his left.

Those who passed by derided him, shaking their heads and saying, "You who would destroy the temple and build it in three days, save yourself! If you are the Son of God, come down from the cross." In the same way the chief priests...with the scribes and elders, were mocking him, saying, "He saved others; he cannot save himself. He is the King of Israel; let him come down from the cross now, and we will believe in him. He trusts in God; let God deliver him now, if he wants to; for he said, 'I am God's Son.'" The bandits who were crucified with him also taunted him in the same way.

From noon on, darkness came over the whole land until three in the afternoon. And about three o'clock Jesus cried with a loud voice, "Eli, Eli, lema sabachthani?" that is, "My God, my God, why have you forsaken me?" When some of the bystanders heard it, they said, "This man is calling for Elijah." At once one of them ran and got a sponge, filled it with sour wine, put it on a stick, and gave it to him to drink. But the others said, "Wait, let us see whether Elijah will come to save him."

Then Jesus cried again with a loud voice and breathed his last.

Matthew 27:31b-50

27. Mary: Mother of Sorrows

**STANDING NEAR THE CROSS OF JESUS [WAS] HIS
MOTHER.**

Mary is not present at the triumphant entry of Jesus
into Jerusalem, but she is present—under the cross—
at the decisive hour of the redemption of the world.
More than a mother suffers at childbirth, Mary suffers
on hearing the words of anguish from Jesus: *"My God,
my God, why have you forsaken me?"* (MATTHEW 27:46).
No less shaken in heart than Jesus is, she is also one
with him when he entrusts himself totally into the hands
of his Father. During the passion and death of Jesus,
Mary lives the pain. With Jesus, she suffers on behalf of
our sins. She suffers in redemptive compassion. Her
sorrow expresses faith and love. It is a sign of her role
in the new family in which everyone knows the law of
Christ: to bear one another's burdens.

United with Christ, Mary bears our burdens. It is not
that Jesus' suffering would not be complete without
Mary's sufferings. On the contrary, it is the overflowing
power of Christ's death and Resurrection that gives, first
to Mary and then to all the disciples of Christ, the power
to share in his saving solidarity. When we call Mary the
new Eve, or deaconess of salvation, this in no way
denies that Christ alone is our Mediator, our Savior, our
Redeemer. Rather, it accentuates the superabundance
of Christ's suffering, death, and Resurrection. It offers
praise and thanksgiving to him who allows us to be
humble sharers in his work of redemption. Thus we
can offer thanksgiving even for our frustrations and
sufferings. It is not thanksgiving for suffering as such,
but for the transfiguration of suffering and death in sav-

ing solidarity with the death and Resurrection of Christ. And our share cannot be understood without fully acknowledging the privileged share of Mary.

Whatever may be our active share in the mystery of redemption, it is always the result of the passion, death, and Resurrection of our Lord Jesus Christ. And we shall never forget the special share which Mary has had and continues to have in this great mystery.

Blessed are we if we bear one another's burdens in saving solidarity with Mary and our Holy Redeemer.

O sorrowful Mother of Jesus,
you are blessed,
for your suffering
was not like that of those who are caught
in the web of social evil
and the emptiness of a selfish world.
Yours was a suffering
similar to that of Christ.
You, who have suffered with faith,
with hope,
and with love
for all of us,
pray for us
that we may,
with you,
follow Christ on the way of the cross.

The Resurrection

EARLY ON THE FIRST DAY

of the week, while it was still dark, Mary Magdalene came to the tomb and saw that the stone had been removed from the tomb. So she ran and went to Simon Peter and the other disciple, the one whom Jesus loved, and said to them, "They have taken the Lord out of the tomb, and we do not know where they have laid him."

Then Peter and the other disciple set out and went toward the tomb. The two were running together, but the other disciple outran Peter and reached the tomb first. He bent down to look in and saw the linen wrappings lying there, but he did not go in. Then Simon Peter came, following him, and went into the tomb. He saw the linen wrappings lying there, and the cloth that had been on Jesus' head, not lying with the linen wrappings but rolled up in a place by itself. Then the other disciple, who reached the tomb first, also went in, and he saw and believed; for as yet they did not understand the scripture, that he must rise from the dead. Then the disciples returned to their homes.

But Mary stood weeping outside the tomb. As she wept, she bent over to look into the tomb; and she saw two angels in white, sitting where the body of Jesus had been lying, one at the head and the other at the feet. They said to her, "Woman, why are you weeping?" She said to them, "They have taken away my Lord, and I do not know where they have laid him."

When she had said this, she turned around and saw

Jesus standing there, but she did not know that it was Jesus. Jesus said to her, "Woman, why are you weeping? Whom are you looking for?" Supposing him to be the gardener, she said to him, "Sir, if you have carried him away, tell me where you have laid him, and I will take him away."

Jesus said to her, "Mary!" She turned and said to him in Hebrew, "Rabbouni!" (which means Teacher). Jesus said to her, "Do not hold on to me, because I have not yet ascended to the Father. But go to my brothers and say to them, 'I am ascending to my Father and your Father, to my God and your God.'" Mary Magdalene went and announced to the disciples, "I have seen the Lord"; and she told them that he had said these things to her.

John 20:1-18

28. Mary's Easter Joy

ALLELUIA, ALLELUIA!

How is it possible that the texts of the gospels mention the Easter faith of so many others but not that of Mary, the mother of Jesus? Perhaps because the gospels underline two aspects: first, the belief that Christ is truly risen and has revealed himself; and second, the fact that the disciples came only gradually to the fullness of belief.

Mary had fully lived the exodus with her son; she shared the depth of his mystery with him. Thus she was not faced with the difficulties Peter, Mary Magdalene, and the disciples of Emmaus had in coming to a belief in Resurrection. Mary, our spiritual mother, is the model of the Easter faith of the whole Church. Intimately united with the suffering and death of Jesus, she is equally united with the joy of his Resurrection. The closer we imitate her, the greater will be our Easter joy, and the simpler our path to fullness of faith.

The gospels present us with a number of other women who, even before the apostles, came to faith in Jesus Christ. John's Gospel pays particular attention to Mary Magdalene's path of faith. She too, in her own way, is a model of our faith, insofar as our faith needs further purification, greater clarity, and strength. Mary Magdalene seeks and finds Jesus because of her great love, although the full light of faith does not break through at once. Both Mary, the mother of Jesus, and Mary Magdalene should be subjects of our meditation: the innocent faith of maturity on one hand, and faith still in need of search and purification on the other.

Easter day in the gospels emphasizes the role of

women. Mary, the queen of the apostles, is *the* woman. She is the one who, with all her being, sings the Song of the Servant and the joy of the Resurrection. At her side are other women, who in the depth of their faith aid in the apostolic work of the Twelve. And, at the heart of the Church, there are—with Mary—all those who believe in the risen Lord and spread this faith with all their being.

Blessed are we if, in imitation of Mary, our Easter joy lasts all year.

O Mary,
blessed are you
for you have believed
that God's promise will be fulfilled.
Blessed are you
in your Easter joy,
rejoicing
in the faith of the apostles
and in the faith of so many humble people.
Pray for us
that we seek
first of all
a living, grateful faith,
a faith
that bears fruit in love and justice
for the salvation of the world,
a faith
that brings all to know Jesus Christ,
the Son of the living God,
whom we have the honor to call your son.

Pentecost

WHEN THE DAY OF PENTECOST HAD COME, they were all together in one place. And suddenly from heaven there came a sound like the rush of a violent wind, and it filled the entire house where they were sitting. Divided tongues, as of fire, appeared among them, and a tongue rested on each of them. All of them were filled with the Holy Spirit and began to speak in other languages, as the Spirit gave them ability.

Now there were devout Jews from every nation under heaven living in Jerusalem. And at this sound the crowd gathered and was bewildered, because each one heard them speaking in the native language of each. Amazed and astonished, they asked, "Are not all these who are speaking Galileans? And how is it that we hear, each of us, in our own native language? Parthians, Medes, Elamites, and residents of Mesopotamia, Judea and Cappadocia, Pontus and Asia, Phrygia and Pamphylia, Egypt and the parts of Libya belonging to Cyrene, and visitors from Rome, both Jews and proselytes, Cretans and Arabs—in our own languages we hear them speaking about God's deeds of power." All were amazed and perplexed, saying to one another, "What does this mean?" But others sneered and said, "They are filled with new wine."

Acts 2:1-13

29. **Mary and the Holy Spirit**

ALL THESE WERE CONSTANTLY DEVOTING THEMSELVES
TO PRAYER, TOGETHER WITH CERTAIN WOMEN, INCLUD-
ING MARY THE MOTHER OF JESUS, AS WELL AS HIS
BROTHERS.

Mary, who since the great moment of redemption
has also become the mother of John and of us all, is
with the apostles at the great event of Pentecost. She
lives her role in the new family of God which is repre-
sented by the apostles, the holy women, and some of
her relatives who followed her in faith. Her prayer and
her presence among the apostles is essential for the
preparation of the pentecostal event.

Mary is indispensable for our life of prayer and our
path to faith. The powerful coming of the Holy Spirit is
prepared by the prayer and expectation of Mary, and of
the whole community with her: *All of them were filled
with the Holy Spirit.* The power of the Holy Spirit gives
full life to the Church of the paschal faith in a new Pentecost. Openness to the Spirit is always a gift of Christ,
the new Adam. It can, therefore, never be separated from
Mary's role as the new Eve, the mother of the living.

Never under the law of sin, Mary lives fully, knowing
the liberating law of the Spirit that unites her with Jesus,
the One anointed by the Holy Spirit. More than all the
others saved by Jesus Christ, Mary bears *the fruit of the
Spirit [which] is love, joy, peace, patience, kindness,
generosity, faithfulness, gentleness, and self-control*
(GALATIANS 5:22-23A).

Mary continuously invites us to an intensive life of
prayer, to trust in the Lord, to praise and give thanks,
and thus to be faithful to the covenant. An authentic

devotion to Mary goes hand in hand with a confirmed faith in the Holy Spirit and an increasing docility toward the gift of grace. When we love and venerate Mary, and adore the Holy Spirit with her, we are enabled to live the new law, manifested in the Eucharist. We consequently consider the gifts of the Spirit, together with the needs of our brothers and sisters, as the highest law. This belongs to the very essence of the new birth in Christ and the ongoing spiritual renewal of the Church.

Blessed are we when we bear the fruit of the Holy Spirit, living faithfully under the law of God.

O Mary,
you were the heart of the Church
when the apostles awaited
and experienced
the powerful coming of the Holy Spirit.
Pray for us
that we may ever more completely understand
and experience
what it means
to believe in
and adore
the Holy Spirit
together with the Father
and the Son.